# A Pictorial History
# of Brixworth

A village view taken from the grounds of Brixworth Hall sometime
between 1910 and 1920 looking north with the parish church of All
Saints' rising high above the rooftops in the background. Built around
680 A.D. this famous church is not only the oldest building in Brixworth,
but is believed to be the largest surviving Anglo-Saxon building in the
country. It has been in continuous use as a centre of Christian worship for
over 1300 years. It is a Grade I Listed Building, being of exceptional
architectural and historical interest.

COMPILED BY BRIXWORTH HISTORY SOCIETY
SUPPORTED BY ILMOR ENGINEERING LIMITED

## Front and Back Cover Illustration

A view looking east along Church Street, c1907, showing The Market or Butter Cross in the foreground with Roe Charity School building (now All Saints' Heritage Centre) behind. Further along on the right is the Hare & Hounds public house which became a private residence after it closed for business in 1953. The site of the Market Cross dates back to 1268 when the village was granted a weekly market and annual fair by Henry III. When one elderly resident was asked recently if she was one of the three children in this photograph sitting on the steps of the Market Cross she replied 'Oh no dear, we were not allowed to play down there, that was the rough end of the village!'

# *A Pictorial History*
# *of Brixworth*

FOREWORD BY RACHEL WATSON
COUNTY ARCHIVIST - NORTHAMPTONSHIRE RECORD OFFICE

Looking through this collection of photographs, from the middle of the last century to the last decade of this, I can only wonder at the great changes 120 years have brought. Look at the unmade roads in some of the photographs and then think of what is there now, including a bypass. All the changes are captured here 'forever' in a beautifully prepared book, along with information, which has only been available, to date, in oral history. I do not wonder, however, that it has been produced by the Brixworth History Society. It is a Society that thrives on the dedication of its members to the place in which they live. They are also dedicated to doing things; this, after all, is their third publication.

I think that the organisation behind the Society should also be noted. Societies of all sorts are made up of members and those who organise. There cannot be one without the other. The co-operative effort was evident both at the first meeting of the Society when I was the guest speaker and again when I had the pleasure of opening their first exhibition in 1991. On this occasion someone's forethought, or rotten sense of humour, had organised local piper John Walker to pipe me to the platform where I was to officially open the exhibition. The only thing that I had not been instructed to say or do that evening was to wear a kilt, but by happy co-incidence I happened to be wearing one!

The Society has continued to grow since its launch in 1990. Long may it thrive - to record the past which has changed so markedly, and to record, also, the present, when our surroundings and people themselves seem to be in a constant state of motion. The work carried out by Brixworth History Society is invaluable.

COMPILED AND PUBLISHED BY BRIXWORTH
HISTORY SOCIETY IN 1999

ISBN 0–9536010–0–5

The production team has made every effort to ensure the information
contained in this publication is accurate. Most of the text has been
compiled using recollections of Brixworth residents, supplemented by
information extracted from articles written by others. As you view these
images of the past you may well find that you disagree with some of the
text or feel you could add more to that which has been written.
If this is the case please let the production team know, as this will
ensure the records kept by the History Society are as accurate and
comprehensive as humanly possible.

TYPESET IN GALLIARD & NUPTIAL SCRIPT BY ARMADILLO,
NORTHAMPTON

PRINTED IN GREAT BRITAIN BY
THE DIRECT PRINTING COMPANY LIMITED
6 STAVELEY WAY, BRIXWORTH, NORTHAMPTON NN6 9TX

# CONTENTS

A charming early 20th century photograph of three young children sitting on the steps of the Market or Butter Cross in Church Street with The Granary, one of Brixworth's oldest surviving houses, on the right. By 1912 the buildings in the background on the left had been replaced by Brixworth's first purpose built fire station which remained at this site on Cross Hill until the early 1930's when the village fire brigade was disbanded. An Auxiliary Fire Service was set up prior to the Second World War located on the Northampton Road next to the original Blason's Garage. The present fire station on the Holcot Road was opened in 1953.

## INTRODUCTION

# A Pictorial History of Brixworth

For almost a decade Brixworth History Society has built up an extensive collection of photographs depicting more than a century of the village's history. These photographs provide a unique pictorial insight into Brixworth's recent past and we hope that those we have carefully selected and reproduced in this book give you, the reader, an opportunity to capture and enjoy some of the village's rich heritage and social history. As you flick through the pages that follow, please remember that most of the photographs you see are copies of originals taken by local people, with very few the work of professional photographers. It is also worth noting that nearly all of the images you are about to look at have been reproduced without changing the content or quality of the originals.

To try and reflect the time span covered by the photographs held by the Society's archivist, we have included what we believe to be one of the earliest surviving pictures taken in Brixworth dating from 1856 alongside several photographs that were 'snapped' a few years before this book went into print. The 1856 picture reproduced on page 46 is one of the Society's prized treasures.

We are pleased to record our gratitude to the five organisations that have sponsored this edition of 'A Pictorial History of Brixworth', especially as four of them have companies located in the village. Firstly to **Ilmor Engineering Ltd**, initially for their interest and confidence in our concept of the book, and subsequently for their generosity in financing all of the production costs. Their contribution has been recognised in the 'Brixworth at Work' section on pages 23-25, with a short history of the company alongside four photographs illustrating the growth of their facilities within the village's location. Our appreciation also goes to **Ashbourne Pharmaceuticals, Haddonstone Ltd, Rigiflex Extrusions Ltd,** and **Unit 2 Glass Limited of Corby** for their individual donations which have been used to pay for the book's preparation work and its launch. This book could not have been published without their collective support. We also value the specialised technical advice that we have received from our printers **The Direct Printing Company Ltd. of Brixworth** regarding the format of the book and numerous other pre-production matters. Our grateful thanks to them all.

The Society's main aim, now it has become an established historical organisation, is to have its own building in Brixworth in which it can display and share with others the growing number of village photographs, artifacts and items of memorabilia it has been given. All the income received from the sale of this book will bring the Society a little closer to having the necessary funds to realise this ambition. Thank you for your support.

**Production Team ~ John Dawkins ~ Mandy Dawkins ~ Pauline Kirton ~ Susan Mallard**

Local residents Mrs. Evans and Mr. Lade standing outside Brixworth's Provident Co-operative Society store situated on the corner of Church Street and Silver Street around the time of the First World War. Access to a bakehouse was through the half open gate on the right of this picture and it was here where 'Baker Nicholls', the village baker, would cook Yorkshire puddings for locals on Sunday mornings. The Co-operative Society has had premises in the village since 1869 and in 1914 it bought the corner shop leading into South View at No 69 Northampton Road and remained there until 1956. In 1935 it opened up another store, this time under its new name of the Northampton Co-operative Society Ltd., on its present site at the corner of Northampton Road and Holcot Road. The Co-op once had a bakehouse at the rear of No 120 Northampton Road.

# Section 1
# Buildings

*Brixworth is blessed with an abundance of important and attractive buildings that have helped shape the village of today. Surprisingly only sixteen of these have been officially identified by the Secretary of State for the Environment as worthy of protection as Listed Buildings because of their exceptional architectural or historic interest. The photographs chosen for this section show some buildings that no longer exist in the village, some that have survived but with an appearance much changed from their original shape and size and others that still look exactly as they did at the time when they were built.*

A remarkable view looking north along Northampton Road in the early 1900's. The first two buildings in the foreground right were believed to have been built in 1876 and formed part of Arthur Trick's farm. They were demolished in the mid 1930's to provide the site for the present day Co-op store. During the last century the buildings along both sides of this narrow part of Northampton Road have been occupied by a variety of businesses including a saddlers, a blacksmiths, a barbers, a greengrocers, a doctor's surgery, a dressmakers, a betting shop, two cycle repair shops and an antiques showroom. Some of the buildings on the right side of the road were moved back when the road was widened in the 1920's and others have completely disappeared. The lady walking towards the camera is passing the George public house, believed to date from the 14th century. In the far distance on the right is the thatched roofed building of the original Red Lion public house before it was knocked down and rebuilt on its present site.

All Saints' Church c1905 taken from The Vicarage garden when the Reverend A. K. Pavey was the incumbent. Parts of The Vicarage date from the late 17th century and the garden was formerly a burial ground. The building ceased to be the home of Brixworth's Vicar in 1975.

Interior view of All Saints' Church taken from a postcard produced around 1910. At this time lighting in the church was provided by the ornate oil lamps seen here in the nave and beyond in the presbytery. Mains electricity used for domestic lighting came to the village in the mid 1930's.

The Northampton Road, Kennel Terrace, Holcot Road crossroads looking north in the early 1900's. On the right, a post outside Green's the Tailors may have been used by residents to tie up their horses before entering one of the nearby shops. Just visible, in the far distance, are the signs for The George and The Red Lion public houses. The 17th century building in the centre, with two workmen on the roof, was, about the time of this photograph, the home and workshop of a local blacksmith. In 1914 the premises became the village post office and general store and since 1980, a restaurant and private residence.

The same crossroads in the early 1900's, this time looking south. The trees on the left are on land once used as a cricket pitch, a tennis court and a rifle range owned by 'Old Man Preston' and now occupied by the Lone Pine Court flats. Since this photograph was taken several of the private houses on the right have been converted into shops.

Brixworth Hall, set in its extensive grounds, around 1905. The original house was built in 1595 by Edward Saunders of Welford whose father had built The Manor House, on the Harborough Road, fifteen years earlier. Considerable remodelling of The Hall took place during the 18th and 19th centuries. Lived in at various times by several Lords of the Manor and High Sheriffs of Northamptonshire, the building was eventually demolished in 1954. All that remain today are the lake and stable block, which like the rest of the grounds, form part of a private housing development.

The Manor House in the early 1900s. Built in 1580 by the Saunders family on a site previously occupied by a 12th Century moated manor. One of Brixworth's sixteen listed buildings, The Manor House possesses a magnificent spiral staircase with a newel post that rises from the cellar to the top of the house.

The austere looking Brixworth Union Workhouse, Spratton Road, as it was in the early part of the 20th century. The Workhouse opened at a cost of £5,800 on March 25th 1837 ready to accommodate 265 inmates. It closed its doors for the last time in 1935 when some of the building was converted into offices for the Rural District Council.

The Rural District Council Offices, Spratton Road sometime before their closure in 1974. The offices occupied what remained of the Union Workhouse after it closed in 1935. The council homes beyond the main building in this photograph were demolished during the 1970s and the land eventually used for private houses and a purpose built Library and Community Centre which was opened by Neil Kinnock, an E.U. Commissioner in 1999.

The junction of High Street turning left into Church Street and Silver Street leading off to the right in the 1920's. Notice the public house sign of The Crown hanging from the upper story of the building in the centre of the picture. All Saints' Church rises high above the roofline. The bay windowed house on the right was rebuilt after it burned down during renovation work in 1976.

A late 1940's view looking west along Church Street. Beyond the Market or Butter Cross is The Granary, one of Brixworth's many impressive private houses. Believed to date from the reign of Charles 1, The Granary was, for a time, used as a nursing home. Many of the buildings on the right, beyond the parked car, have been demolished and replaced with later buildings. Rookery Farmhouse (known by many as Fox's Farmhouse) can be seen in the distance on the corner of the right turn into Station Road.

The original Roe Charity School, Church Street, built in 1811. This photograph was taken immediately before it was purchased by the Friends of All Saints' Church who began work to restore it in 1993. The building is now used as a meeting place and exhibition centre for church organisations and other parish groups. Beyond and to the right is a glimpse of the former late 19th century village primary school now functioning as Brixworth Community Centre.

The Methodist Chapel, Church Street before its conversion into a private residence during the 1970s. Referred to in Kelly's Directory as a Wesleyan Chapel it was built in 1811 and extended in 1860. For many years the Brixworth Methodist group was responsible for organising the village May Queen celebrations.

A late 1940's or early 1950's winter's scene looking up Church Street towards Rookery Farm (once the home of farmer William George Fox) on the junction with Station Road leading off to the left. The small brick building above the wall on the left was a boot repair shop before it was demolished. The hounds, belonging to the Pytchley Hunt, were kept at this time in kennels in Kennel Terrace. Rookery Farm was demolished in 1958.

An early 20th century photograph taken from Froghall of The Rookery, Church Street (when it was the home of the Bucknall family) and showing barns dating from 1726. A former resident of The Rookery and one of the owners of Brixworth Hall, William Wood Esq., was murdered by Major Thomas Isham in the Hall on October 5th 1854.

An early 20th century photograph of one of Brixworth's remaining three public houses, The Coach & Horses to the north of the village on the Harborough Road (the landlady at the time was Mrs. Emily Eaton). Dating back to the early 1700's The Coach & Horses provided the first change of horses for stage coaches heading north out of Northampton. The inn was renowned for the speed at which horses and harnesses were changed, a team of four replaced in under four minutes, a record for the north bound route.

Next to The Coach & Horses is the ivy covered Pound House as seen in this picture dating from c1914. Situated opposite the main entrance to the grounds of Brixworth Hall, The Pound House is an impressive Grade II listed buildings bearing a 1594 datestone. Originally a farm house it was extended in 1709 and has had various names including Ivy House, when this photograph was taken, Eaglehurst and Harwood House.

An unusual view of the Village Hall and Parish Hall in 1934, showing the Holcot Road stretching steeply upwards from it's junction with Northampton Road. The Village Hall has been refurbished several times since it opened in 1928 and is currently undergoing further improvements. The Northampton Co-operative Society opened a store on the land behind the wooden fence previously occupied by a farmhouse. The farm buildings and houses stretching up the Holcot Road have disappeared, with part of the site eventually being used for the store's car park.

The site of today's Co-op store captured on film some time after it opened its doors for the first time in 1935. Photographic evidence that the road and path outside the store had recently been dug up may have been due to the arrival of mains water in the village in 1936. (Some things never change!)

Harry and Ted Green standing outside their tailors shop on the corner of Northampton Road and Holcot Road, sometime before 1920. Mr. H. Grainger, one of the employees, who worked for the Greens, can be seen peering through the half opened door on the left. The family business was started in Brixworth by John Green in the 1870's.

A busy scene in Kennel Terrace during a summer's day in the early 1900's. This delightful row of stone cottages originally housed some of the Pytchley Hunt staff and the three storey homes are still occupied. The wall of the two storey cottages, with the windows filled in, has also survived to this day as part of a workshop once used for the restoration of traction engines.

An early 20th century view looking along Newlands towards Northampton Road. Buildings to note are the high sided walls of The Grange on the right hand side and The Brown House beyond the low wall on the left, which was once a farm house belonging to The Wood's estate. The pub sign on The Fox & Hounds ale house can just be seen in the distant right. This particular ale house, one of several in Brixworth that have subsequently closed, dates back to 1884.

A view looking along Silver Street in the 1920's taken from its junction with High Street and Church Street. The two girls are standing outside Brixworth's Co-op store on the left, and the pub sign to The Fox and Pheasant can just be seen in the distance on the right side of the street.

A copy of an original colour photograph taken in 1994 of The Grange in Kennel Terrace. Believed to have originally been two 18th century farm cottages this tall and imposing building was used to house German prisoners of war. From the early 1900's until the 1940's Captain Frank Litchfield, the secretary to the Pytchley Hunt, lived here.

A peaceful scene looking north along the Northampton Road sometime after 1912. The first building on the left, partly obscured behind the trees, had been operating as Highfield Laundry from 1906 under its proprietress Mrs. Fonge. The present owners of this property, Rigiflex Extrusions Ltd, purchased the premises in the early 1970's and set up their business manufacturing plastic components. The three large family houses below Highfield House were built between 1896 and 1906 and are still occupied today.

A 1924 photograph of The Hare & Hounds public house in Church Street. Listed as a fully licensed premises from 1847 The Hare & Hounds sold Phipps beer brewed in Northampton and one of its landlords, Fred Rose, used his horse and cab to transport people to Brixworth station.

A remarkable view of The Red Lion public house, with its thatched roof and distinctive chimney stacks, some time before 1928 when it was demolished and rebuilt on its present site set back from the sharp bend on the Northampton Road. At the turn of the century long carts had to be man handled and 'bump turned' to get them round the 'Red Lion corner'. The wall and overhanging trees beyond The Red Lion belong to the grounds of Brixworth Hall.

# Section 2
# Brixworth at Work

At the beginning of the 20th century the largest employers in Brixworth were the Pytchley Hunt, the ironstone quarrying company Attenborough & Timms and the owners of the ten local farms. It is fitting, therefore, that the majority of photographs selected for this section of the book depict images from these three major forms of local employment. The opening of the village's first industrial estate in the late 1970's signalled the emergence of manufacturing and service industries as the village's largest employers, with several large national and international companies basing themselves in Brixworth. One such company was Ilmor Engineering who is the main sponsor of this book. In recognition of its generous support this section begins with a brief history of the formation and growth of this world famous company.

Ilmor Engineering design and manufacture CART and Formula One racing engines for Mercedes-Benz. The company was started in 1984 by Brixworth resident and Cosworth employee, Paul Morgan and his colleague Mario Illien. The two of them decided to set up their own engine manufacturing plant and chose Brixworth as an ideal location for their venture, primarily because they wanted a site in close proximity to Paul's house. The industrial site also had favourable commercial rates and was close to an excellent road network. They first utilised existing facilities in the village for their venture like the old Union Workhouse/Council Offices building on the Spratton Road where they began the design of their first engine whilst the first Ilmor factory unit was built on the Quarry Road industrial estate (see the photograph on page 24). Since that time Ilmor has continued to expand its facilities and now occupies 10,854 square metres of land and employs over 400 people, of which 40 are 'Brixworthians'.

Following continued race and Championship wins, both in the CART and Formula One series, Ilmor has established a reputation as one of the finest race-engine design companies in the world. This has been achieved through the good location of facilities and a dedicated workforce. As part of local industry, Ilmor is committed to continuing its success in motor racing and to providing employment and support to Brixworth and the surrounding areas.

In 1984 Paul Morgan and Mario Illien bought this three acre site at the end of Quarry Road on which they built their first factory unit. This land originally formed part of Brixworth's Woods South ironstone quarry. 'October House' on the horizon (now demolished) stood on the Holcot Road with Brixworth to the right and Pitsford Reservoir and the village of Holcot three miles to the left.

Ilmor's first factory unit completed in 1985 which occupied only 604 square metres. The design and manufacture of the first Ilmor built CART engine took place here with the Chevrolet Indy V8 engine. This engine won Ilmor's first CART race in 1987 and a total of 86 races out of 123 entered.

A very different picture, this time an aerial shot showing the Ilmor site in 1997 with Brixworth's by-pass (opened in 1989) at the bottom of the photograph. By this time Ilmor had expanded their site following continued success in both Formula One and CART Championships and their partnership with Mercedes-Benz in 1993.

One of Ilmor's racing engines - the 1998 Mercedes-Benz FO110G V10. This Ilmor designed and built engine powered the McLaren-Mercedes team to winning the Formula One Drivers' and Constructors' World Championship. This win extended Ilmor's many other Championship wins and Indianapolis 500 victories in the CART series.

Ironstone workers in the early 1930's from the Woods South pit immediately behind the Manor House on the Harborough Road with Brixworth No 1 locomotive in the background. The rough and extremely dangerous working conditions at this time bred thirsty men and it is not surprising that their noisy and sometimes drunken behaviour resulted in the top end of Silver Street being referred to as 'Hell Corner' by nearby residents.

Another group of ironstone workers, this time from the 1920's, gathered together for a 'team' photograph on the quarry site north of All Saints' Church. The men assembled above the engine were known as top runners and they had the job of moving soil in barrows from one side of the pit to the other along the narrow pitch pine planks. This particular task was referred to as 'running the top'. Some of the workers can be seen sitting and standing on these planks in this picture.

Engine driver Charlie Gubbins with workmate and ironstone blacksmith Fred Booker, standing alongside Hunslet locomotive Louisa near to Brixworth station in 1939. Louisa was purchased by quarry owners Attenborough & Timms in 1900 and was last seen pulling wagons in the Clay Cross yard in July 1947. Most of the ironstone workers lived in Brixworth with a few walking to work from the surrounding villages.

A spectacular view captured during the late afternoon of March 5th 1954 showing the aerial ropeway crossing that served the Lamport ironstone quarries passing over the Northampton to Market Harborough Road north of Brixworth. The photographer's Francis Barnett 197cc motorcycle can be seen parked on the right of the picture.

A 1920's photograph of the Duke of York, later George VI (centre), with the Pytchley Hunt in Kennel Terrace. The Duke of York and his brother the Duke of Windsor hunted with the Pytchley and often visited Huntsman Frank Freeman in his cottage in Spratton Road. Frank started work for the Pytchley in 1906 taking over from Will Goodall and John Isaac.

Huntsman Frank Freeman (foreground, centre) leading a meeting of the Pytchley Hunt in the grounds of Brixworth Hall in the 1920's. The greatest honour for Frank, during his 25 years working for the Hunt, came when he introduced the present Queen Elizabeth to hunting when she was a young Princess.

First and second kennel men with the hounds outside the Pytchley Hunt horse stables on the north side of Kennel Terrace in 1908. The stone wall remains to this day forming part of 'The Mews' housing development. During its heyday the Pytchley owned 50 pairs of hounds and almost 60 horses.

An early 1900's photograph of the Pytchley Hunt hounds with the first and second kennel men outside their kennels on the south side of Kennel Terrace. These kennels were considered to be some of the best in the country being light, airy and warm; features much appreciated by the men who worked in them and the dogs they cared for.

The workforce of Green Brothers photographed in 1905 outside their place of work on the junction of Northampton Road and Holcot Road. At this time most of the employees were local people although several of those seen here travelled daily from Northampton.

Frank Green at work measuring cloth inside his tailor's shop sometime before 1935. Notice the roofline of buildings in Kennel Terrace through the large window behind Mr. Green and the gable end of Trick's farmhouse that stood on the corner of Holcot Road, visible on the right hand side of the window above the open order book.

A photograph believed to be of local builder, carpenter and undertaker James Bray, with his wife, standing outside his premises in Froghall in 1900. This building now forms part of an extended private residence. The Bray family name appears in Brixworth's trade directories from 1884 through to the 1970's.

Brixworth stonewall builders Alfred Bull (left) and Jack Dawson (right), with colleague Trevor Shaw from Brington, working for Northamptonshire Council in Watford Village during 1978.

Hedge layer Walter Wootton at work on Park Farm, Spratton Road c1936. It is reported that Walter and his wife shared the same clay pipe. Known locally as 'Jump up Jesus', Walter lived in Church Street and was a keen supporter of local football.

Thatcher John Buswell, known by his friends as 'Thatcher Jack' and wearing his familiar flat cap, at work on the roof of the Pytchley Hunt horse stables in Kennel Terrace during the 1940's. The kennels and the hunt staff moved to their present quarters on Station Road in September 1966.

A copy taken from a colour photograph of local engineer Phil Foreman and his son Robbie with their beautifully decorated 1917 Fowler 14321 traction engine 'The Yorkshire Belle' outside the Village Hall d u r i n g B r i x w o r t h H i s t o r y Society's 1991 Exhibition.

Carrier/carter Samuel 'Chippy' Tyrrell seen here outside The Vine public house on Station Road in the 1920's. 'Chippy' was often seen with a cab, owned by Fred Rose the landlord of the Hare & Hounds in Church Street, transporting villagers to and from Brixworth Station. The horse in this picture is believed to be Bowler who would never pass the Red Lion Inn in Newlands without stopping!

Local farm owner Frank Lever and farm worker Jim Carter seen here threshing on Folly Farm, Spratton Road in 1932. At this time there were 16 farms in and around the parish of Brixworth with over half covering 150 acres or more.

A summer's day in 1920 on Grange Farm, Holcot Road with Bill and Arthur Cockerill on top of the hay cart, George Williams to the left, Mrs. Walters about to toss up more hay and farm owner Jim Rose. Jim's son Ron still lives at Grange Farm with its spectacular views overlooking Pitsford Reservoir.

Women's Land Army girls Joyce Amer, left and Violet Gibson at Park Farm in 1947. Joyce and her family were evacuated from London when she was 18 and moved into a bungalow in Eastfield Road. All of Joyce's working life was spent at Park Farm on Spratton Road, being employed for much of the time in the dairy.

Bill Marsh and Ray Plain with horse Blue Peter at Park Farm c1956. The horse was often very vicious and for everyone's safety had to be kept muzzled. The farmhouse at Park Farm was built in 1891.

Ploughing in progress near to Spratton Station with Stanley Baldwin driving a half track Fordson tractor c1950 when he worked on Park Farm for the Turney brothers. Stan eventually set up his own milk delivery business supplying customers in Brixworth and surrounding villages.

From the left, Sub-postmaster Joseph Hardwick and Mrs. Hardwick, Daisy Harris, No Name, Mr. Summerfield and Mr. Pearce outside Brixworth Post Office in Kennel Terrace in 1918. Mr. Pearce pushed his Post Office handcart every day to the neighbouring villages of Hanging Houghton, Lamport and Draughton calling at the farms and often running errands for people along the way.

# Section 3
## People

The population of Brixworth almost doubled from 1601 to the beginning of the 20th century, reaching 1123 at the time of the 1901 census. A substantial increase in the number of new properties built within the parish during the late 1900's will result in the village becoming home to well in excess of 5000 inhabitants by the beginning of the 21st century. Like most communities, Brixworth has had its fair share of local personalities and nationally famous residents. Well known visitors to the parish over the centuries have included members of the Royal Family, Members of Parliament, religious leaders and celebrities from the worlds of sport and entertainment. The photographs of local people associated with the village that have been included in this section are a small selection taken from the many thousands of individuals and groups of people who have made a contribution to Brixworth's social history.

Four happy Brixworth couples outside All Saints Church in June 1996 after reaffirming their wedding vows at a special service conducted by The Reverend Anthony Watkins. From the left, Jack and Winifred Dawson, Cyril and Margaret Pratt, Druscilla and Donald Copson and Harry and Peggy Mallard. Remarkably, two years after the photograph was taken all four couples had celebrated their diamond wedding anniversary (more wedding photographs can be seen in Section 7 starting on page 89).

The Reverend Alfred Katenbeck Pavey M.A., Vicar of All Saints' Church from 1896 to 1917. He died following a mosquito bite while on holiday in Scotland in 1923. He was instrumental in raising considerable sums of money for the restoration of the church and the preservation of the church school.

The Reverend Nicholas Chubb, Vicar of Brixworth from 1969 to 1981, photographed at St. Mary and All Saints' Church, Holcot. Nicholas Chubb was the last Vicar to live in the stonebuilt vicarage by the church and the first to use the new brick built vicarage on Station Road. It was also during his time at Brixworth that the church celebrated its 1300th anniversary.

A group photograph taken outside Brixworth Hall c1910, possibly showing local members of a political party. Seated on the front row 6th, 7th, 8th and 9th from the left are the wife of the Vicar of Brixworth, her husband The Reverend A. K. Pavey, Mrs. Paget and her husband Major Guy Paget.

John 'Lumpy' Green with his family. John started his tailoring business 'Green Brothers' in Brixworth in 1870. Employing up to 20 workers and supplying clothes for seven hunts the shop closed for business in the village in December 1953 and moved to Market Harborough.

A 1926 photograph of the diminutive 'Jiggery' Teeton taken outside his place of work at Greens the Tailors on the corner of Northampton Road and Holcot Road.

Mr. Coulson, area manager of milking machinery company Alfa Laval, right, presenting Harvey Wykes, left, with a silver milking liner to mark the opening of the first abreast milking parlour in Northamptonshire at Park Farm, Spratton Road in 1961. Proud farm manager Guy Kipling is seen looking on.

Local farm labourer Joseph 'Joey' Cook with horse Joy. Born in 1873, the son of William, also a farm worker and Emma Cook, 'Joey' worked for three generations of the Mallard family (present owner Harry, his father Walter and grandfather James) at Home Farm on Church Street. Joey's family has lived in Brixworth since 1775.

A rare 1862 picture of the 5th Earl Spencer 'The Red Earl' dressed as the Master of the Pytchley Hunt at the age of 27. During his mastership of the hunt, Earl Spencer used the kennels at his home on the Althorp Estate.

A 1908 photograph of Tommy Agutter taken in the yard of the dog kennels in Kennel Terrace when he was the second whipper-in to the Pytchley Hunt under Master Lord Annaly. He eventually became the first whipper-in for huntsman Frank Freeman.

Frank Freeman Huntsman to the Pytchley Hunt from 1906-1931. He, with his Master Lord Annaly, were considered to be one of the best Master and Huntsman combinations in the history of the Hunt. The greatest honour for Frank Freeman was when he introduced Princess Elizabeth (later Queen Elizabeth II) to hunting.

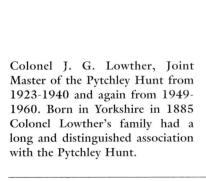

Colonel J. G. Lowther, Joint Master of the Pytchley Hunt from 1923-1940 and again from 1949-1960. Born in Yorkshire in 1885 Colonel Lowther's family had a long and distinguished association with the Pytchley Hunt.

Early 20th century photograph of local children Rosie and Lizzie Watham dressed for their mother's funeral. A few weeks after this picture was taken the two girls were admitted to the Workhouse on the Spratton Road. Following their elementary education at Brixworth School in Church Street, they both went into service.

Richard Corfield Bucknall age 93 years 6 months photographed outside his family home, The Rookery, Church Street just before his death in 1934. The Bucknall family supplied the arum lilies used in the bouquet presented to each year's May Queen. Richard's son Percy also paid for the display of fireworks in the village in 1945 to celebrate the end of the Second World War. During the time when he lived in Brixworth Percy became a director of the P. & O. Shipping Company.

Brixworth bellringers with other local volunteer helpers pause for a break inside All Saints' Church belfry during maintenance work in September 1974. Standing, from the left, Gillian Land, Tony Brunton, George Hamson, Harry Mallard, Bill Brunton, David Hamson, John Brunton with Dick Walker sitting nearest the camera.

# *Brixworth's Lords of the Manor*

There has been a succession of Lords of the Manor in Brixworth since the 12th century. As principal landowners and dignitaries of the parish they have exercised considerable influence in the village with several holding high office both locally and within the county. The last Lord of the Manor to have lived in Brixworth was William Thomas Vere Wayte Wood, a bachelor, who died at his family home, The Manor House, on October 1st 1949. He was survived by a brother Douglas, who took the title until his death, when the Lordship passed to his brother Frederick who had emigrated to Canada. Little is known of the life of Brixworth's 'squire' since the 1960's.

A rare photograph taken in the spring of 1856 showing Brixworth's joint Lords of the Manor, John Vere Isham from Lamport and Thomas Wood from Brixworth. This is the History Society's oldest photograph.

A much clearer image of Thomas Wood from the 1860's. This particular photograph was taken to produce his visiting card, which he used until his death in 1874.

Although the date of this signed calling card photograph is unknown it shows William Thomas Dixie Wayte Wood, Brixworth's Lord of The Manor from 1874 to 1916. Much of Dixie Wood's married life was spent in Ireland where he lived at Banagher Castle.

An imposing photograph of William Thomas Vere Wayte Wood taken in 1937. Referred to by some as 'Squire Wood', William served his country during the Boer War, became High Sheriff for Northamptonshire in 1936 and was a popular Lord of the Manor from 1916 until his death in 1949.

# Section 4
# Brixworth School

*Thomas Roe from Scaldwell died in 1665 and in his will he left land on the Scaldwell Road to support the education of ten poor children from Brixworth and ten from Scaldwell. This bequest was administered by Trustees and in 1811 they provided the funds for Brixworth's first purpose built school on land next to the Market Cross in Church Street. This building, now known as All Saints' Church Heritage Centre, was purchased by the Friends of All Saints in 1993 and completely refurbished prior to its opening in 1995. In 1870 a brick and stone built school, on the opposite side of the road in Church Street, was opened. In 1973 Brixworth's current village Primary school was opened in Froxhill Crescent by the Bishop of Peterborough. A programme of substantial development at the school, particularly during the late 1990's, will increase its capacity to approximately 500 by the beginning of the 21st century. The 'Old School', in Church Street, as it became known, has been converted into a Community Centre.*

A photograph of Brixworth school children taken by Northampton photographer John Powell outside the Roe Charity School building around 1900. Richard Gough Martin was the Headmaster of the Elementary Mixed School at this time and Miss Emily Maria Edey the mistress of the infants. It is not known if these two teachers are the adults standing either side of the door on the back row. Mr. Martin was also the village 'poor rate' collector.

Teacher, Miss M. Hamson (back row on the extreme right) with her class of infants in 1905-6. Children from several long established Brixworth families are shown here including Bert Baldwin, Alec and John Alcock, Violet, Mabel, Holly and Frank Hamson, Jack Saunders, Rose Cook and Frank Tyrrell.

Headteacher Mr. Martin with a group of older pupils in the Elementary School playground in 1919. At this time three large classes used the main school hall and the lighting was sometimes so poor in the afternoons that pupils could not see enough to read their books. Once again there are children here from well known local families including Douglas Pateman, Mabel Valentine, Nellie Mallard and Anne Bray.

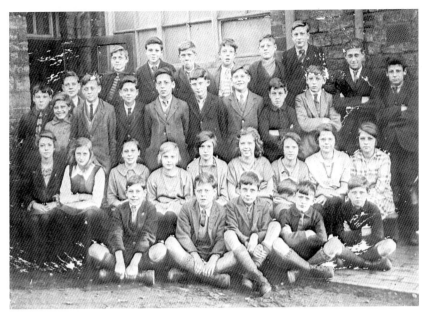

Senior pupils in 1927 including Ron and George Rose, Harry Mallard, Arthur Wright, Stan Eldred, Henry Blason, Marjorie Booker, Jim Dennet, Eric and Cyril Lathbury, Evelyn and Nora Dickens and many more Brixworth teenagers. By the time this photograph was taken the 'earth and pail' toilet system in the school had been replaced by the 'water closet'.

A happy class of infants in the playground with The Granary on Cross Hill in the background on the right. This charming school photograph taken in 1930-31 includes pupils Ken and Cliff Bates and Ron Plowman.

Teacher, Mrs. Moody (second row in the centre) with her class in 1949 including John Blason, Jim Mallard, John Wilson, Peter Eldred, David Rose, Patricia Beck, Carol Kilby, Jim Mallard and Grenville Hughes.

A group of Brixworth School children dressed in costumes specifically designed for their performance in a local drama festival held at Moulton School in 1957.

Senior pupils, smartly dressed in their school uniform, with Headteacher Mr. Ward Hopkins, photographed before they moved to one of Northampton's three Grammar schools or to Moulton Secondary Modern School in 1957.

Happy pupils pose for the photographer during a mid-summer playtime or physical education class in 1957. Several of the children seen here still live in the village.

An 'all male' party of Brixworth pupils and their fathers, waiting to depart from Northampton Castle Station to see England play a Schoolboy's Football International at Wembley sometime in the 1950's. Fathers, on the back row, from the left, Cliff Wicks, Ward Hopkins (Headteacher), Tom Smith, Bob Hughes, Jack Manning, Jack Russell, Mr. Pepper, George Gardiner, Stan Fitzhugh, George Gunnett, Len Hadland and Bill Jones.

Mrs. Battison's Reception class, including Caroline Mabbutt, John Brunton, Stephen Mitton, Martin Hamp and Vincent Manning, working on a variety of tasks during an art lesson at Brixworth School on May 19th 1960.

Another art lesson; this one with Mrs. Joy Hopewell's class in 1961. Pupils seen here include Colin Hayden, Stephen Mabbutt, John Sutton and Peter Billingham.

Teacher Mrs. Hopewell standing on the extreme right of the back row with her Class 2 in 1963. Brixworth children, like those seen here, continued to attend the school in Church Street until the early 1970's when a new school was built on Froxhill Crescent.

Proud members of Brixworth School's football team after winning the Junior Cup in 1962-63. Team members include Richard Lawson, Steven Allen, Mark Callaway, Peter Herman, Tony Brunton, Graham Chapman, Paul Martin, Jeff Armiger and Peter Sharpe.

A relaxing school art lesson around the Market Cross in Church Street, sometime in the 1950's. The familiar sight of The Granary and Mint Cottage can be seen in the background with the Eskimo frozen food depot building behind (later known as All Saints' Cold Store). The old fire station is just visible on the extreme left of the picture.

# Section 5

# Celebrations

Very few communities have the opportunity to celebrate a 1300th anniversary. In 1980 Brixworth residents had such an opportunity when they joined thousands of their friends, guests and visitors in a six month long celebration to mark the 1300th anniversary of the foundation of their parish church of All Saints'. A full and varied Festival programme of events was organised, starting with a special service of thanksgiving on June 5th conducted by the Rt. Reverend F. D. Coggan, the former Archbishop of Canterbury and attended by H.R.H. the Duke of Gloucester and ending on November 1st with a service held in the church conducted by the Lord Bishop of Peterborough. In between these two dates many other specially prepared events took place including a series of concerts and recitals performed by local and national soloists, orchestras and choirs, several talks and exhibitions, a village pageant and craft fair around the Market Cross and stocks and a carnival and fete on the playing fields. The Northampton & County Independent magazine printed a 'Village in Depth' souvenir issue to commemorate this unique anniversary.

Brixworth's first May Queen, Florence Green, seated behind her crown bearer Charles Sharpe in this charming 1914 photograph. Florence can be seen surrounded by many of her friends and their parents on William Preston's land now occupied by the Lone Pine Court flats next to 118 Northampton Road. The village's last May Queen was Victoria Smith who was crowned by Brixworth school teacher Joy Hopewell in 1983. By this time the May Queen had become known as the Rose Queen.

Brixworth's second May Queen Ada Cook with her attendant, her page boy and some of her ladies in waiting, on a decorated dray outside the Union Workhouse on Spratton Road in 1915. At this time the May Queen celebrations started with the crowning on 'Old Man Preston's' land, followed by a procession around the village and finishing with refreshments in the Methodist Chapel in Church Street.

A copy of a post card showing Brixworth's 1915 May Queen Ada Cook again, this time surrounded by her friends, photographed at the crowning ceremony, on the land where Lone Pine Court stands today. The houses in the background on the left are on Northampton Road.

May Queen Grace Malin pictured in 1920 with her bouquet of arum lilies, donated by the Bucknall family who lived at The Rookery. Richard Bucknall and later his son Percy provided the lilies for many of Brixworth's May Queen celebrations.

May Day celebrations in 1921 with May Queen Kathline Hastings in front and on the right of the procession heading down Silver Street. Her attendant Grace Malin is on the left. Most of the buildings in the background have disappeared.

An early 1920's photograph of May Queen Gladys Mills. Gladys was the daughter of Brixworth carrier John Mills who started his business in the village around 1910.

May Queen Hilda James sitting next to the Market Cross in Church Street during the late 1920's. Like many of the early May Queen photographs given to Brixworth History Society, this one is a copy taken from a postcard.

1930 May Queen Marjorie Sturgess, front left, with her attendant Betty Cook at her side outside Brixworth Hall. Behind Marjorie and Betty are nine previous May Queens, from the left, back row, Joan Bates, Florence Green, Nell Cattell, Annie Bray, Grace Malin, middle row, Delia Pateman, Bessie Waters, Hilda James and Kathline Hastings.

May Queen Nancy Tyrrell photographed in 1934 standing outside Green's the Tailors on the corner of Northampton Road and Holcot Road. Immediately behind the group is Tricks farmhouse soon to be demolished to make way for the new Co-op store that opened in 1935.

1939 May Queen Joyce Fox and her attendant Ivy Gubbins, photographed on the footpath alongside one of the two lakes in the grounds of Brixworth Hall. The details of this particular May Queen celebration were obtained from hand written information by Brixworth's Lord of the Manor, William Thomas Vere Wayte Wood, on the reverse of the original photograph.

Sheila Rose the 1940 May Queen seen here holding the large bouquet, standing outside the Orangery at Brixworth Hall. Money collected during all the early May Queen celebrations was given to the National Children's Home and Orphanage.

1941 May Queen Iris Mayes seated in front of the Orangery at Brixworth Hall with her attendant Cynthia Sharpe. This particular year's happy celebration was broadcast on radio to help raise listeners' morale during the Second World War.

Brixworth's 1947 May Queen procession pause for this photograph to be taken on the pavement outside the Red Lion public house. From the left is Rona Dickens, attendant Sylvia Russell, May Queen Joan Rose and Christine Bray. Looking on is Holly Pateman, perhaps unaware she is standing in the middle of Northampton Road, with Betty Rose peering at the camera from behind Christine's garland.

May Queen Maureen Brown with her attendant Prisilla Gubbins and her crown bearer Carol Gubbins, surrounded by their friends in the village hall during their celebrations in 1952.

Carol Kilby crowned Brixworth's May Queen in Queen Elizabeth II's Coronation year 1953. Carol is seen here, with her attendant Maureen Brown, in the grounds of Brixworth Hall with a large Union Jack flag forming an appropriate backdrop.

Brixworth's 'Town Crier' and thatcher John Buswell, dressed in a smock leading the village brass band at the junction of Church Street and Frog Hall during the early 1920's. The procession around the village was organised to raise funds for a new village hall. It was eventually built on the Holcot Road in 1928.

An unknown celebration taking place in the school playground, photographed from the tower of All Saints' Church. Moving from the left to the right along Church Street, across the centre of this picture, are the upper storey windows of The Hare & Hounds public house, the end wall of Percy Vivian's motor engineering premises and the old Thomas Roe school building. In the background are the wooded grounds of Brixworth Hall.

A group of Brixworth ladies, possibly members of the W.I., in fancy dress for the Northampton Hospital Carnival celebrating the coronation of George VI in 1937. The vehicle for this decorated float was provided by local farmer and coal merchant George Hamson.

One of many photographs taken in Brixworth showing how villagers celebrated the end of the Second World War. Here are some of Brixworth's children, resplendent in fancy dress, parading outside a bungalow in St. David's Close. Like many rural communities in the country, Brixworth received large numbers of young evacuees during the war, some of them staying on and settled in the village after peace had been declared.

Two photographs taken in Kennel Terrace that capture the feelings of jubilation and relief in the village on V.E. Day, May 8th 1945, when the people of Brixworth joined the whole country in its celebrations to mark the end of the Second World War. Several of the revellers pictured here can still remember the excitement of the carnival held on the Holcot Road Playing Fields and the many victory parties organised throughout the village.

Members of the congregation performing a scene from a Nativity play staged in All Saints' Church in 1946. Those who took part particularly remember the final performance which was given for prisoners of war being held in the village. Their rendering of 'Silent Night' has never been forgotten.

Members of the choir, pupils from Brixworth School and local residents performing 'A Song of Caedmon', set in Saxon times, in All Saints' Church in 1972. The lyrics for this musical play were written by the well known pianist and entertainer Donald Swann and the costumes were designed and made in the village.

A local majorette group celebrating Queen Elizabeth II's Silver Jubilee in the front garden of a house on Spratton Road in 1977. The houses in the background were demolished soon after this photograph was taken and the land either side of the old Brixworth Union Workhouse building is now the site of Saxon House, Boniface House and the Library/Community Centre.

More village Silver Jubilee celebrations in 1977, this time with Brixworth's own 'Royals' in Hunt Close. From the left, Clare White, Iain Hogg, Jonathan Kirton, Alison Hogg with Alison Kirton clutching her Union Jack flag at the front.

Local schoolchildren enjoy an outdoor rehearsal of 'A Song of Caedmon' outside All Saints' Church during the summer of 1980. The musical play was performed in the church during June as part of the celebrations marking the buildings 1300th Anniversary.

Brixworth resident Mandy Dawkins, with her two children Michael and Julia, appropriately dressed in Saxon costumes, photographed just before joining the village pageant and craft fair around the Butter Cross and Stocks, organised as part of the church's 1300th Anniversary celebrations in June 1980.

Photograph courtesy of Northampton Newspapers Ltd.

Councillor David Kirton receiving the Larger Villages Trophy in the Tidiest Village competition from Earl Spencer on behalf of Brixworth Parish Council. The presentation took place at Hunsbury Hill Farm, Northampton in 1982.

The excitement of balloons being launched at Brixworth Church's Annual Fete held in the churchyard in June 1992. Keeping a watchful eye over the proceedings is the Lord Bishop of Peterborough, The Rt. Reverend Bill Westwood (front centre left). Brixworth was given the royal assent to hold a weekly market and annual fair in the village by Henry III in 1268.

M.P. Roger Freeman cutting the tape as he officially opened Brixworth's By-pass on 27th October 1989. An alternative north/south route to reduce the amount of through traffic on the Northampton to Market Harborough Road was considered for the village back in the 1920's.

Paul Morgan, with his front seat passenger Mario Illien, about to set off along Brixworth's By-pass in his 1927 open-topped 30/98 Vauxhall, accompanied by Dick Walker on his 1913 Triumph motorcycle. These two vintage vehicles and their drivers were the first to use the new road opened in 1989.

# Section 6
# Organisations

In the first Brixworth Village Appraisal book published in November 1994 information was given about the 40 local organisations and sports teams that currently meet and play in Brixworth. One organisation, the Women's Institute, has been active in the village since 1922 and continues to offer its members a varied programme of talks and demonstrations. As you will discover, when you look at the pictures selected for this section, organisations and teams in Brixworth have posed for their group photograph as long ago as the early 1880's. There is clear evidence in several of them that a great deal of time and effort must have been spent to ensure everyone looked their very best for the photographer. Many local sports players have achieved success at some time representing their village in most major team games. Several players have also been selected to represent both their county and their country in their chosen sport. Most of today's village outdoor teams play on the St. David's Recreation Ground which was opened in the mid 1950's. Some of the pitches were laid with top soil taken from fields along the Holcot Road when Pitsford Reservoir was constructed. From the mid 1940's until this time the main sporting venue used for the village's football and cricket teams was on fields belonging to Park Farm immediately behind St. David's Road and Parkfield Road. During the Second World War, football was played on a pitch in the Grange Field (now Pytchley Close). Earlier still, in the 20's and 30's, land beyond what is now The Ashway, along the Holcot Road, provided the pitches for Brixworth's cricket and football teams.

Members of Brixworth's Home Guard photographed outside Brixworth Hall in 1941. The men were under the command of Captain Stanley Barker who was Huntsman to the Pytchley from 1931 until his retirement in 1960. The Home Guard were originally known as the Local Defence Volunteers, or by the nickname of the 'Look, Duck and Vanish Brigade'. At the beginning of the war weapons and uniforms for the men were in short supply so parades in cold weather were not very pleasant.

One of the History Society's oldest photographs dating from 1882 showing the first Band of Hope Group in Brixworth. Little is known of those pictured here other than that they were all members of the local temperance group and that two of the children were related to John Crabb (senior), the Station Master at Spratton.

A rather solemn looking group of smartly dressed local people photographed in the grounds of Brixworth Hall c1910. All those seen here are believed to be members of the Brixworth Pleasant Hour group, with William Thomas Vere Wayte Wood, who became Brixworth's Lord of the Manor in 1916, standing fifth from the right on the back row.

An early 1900's photograph of Brixworth Brass Band taken in the playground of Brixworth School when it was in Church Street. All Saints' Church can be seen in the background. It is believed the band was formed sometime during the 1890's and practised in The Vine public house on Station Road.

A later picture of the village band, this time with the members wearing a smart uniform. The setting for this photograph, like the previous one, is outside the village school when it was in Church Street.

Brixworth Girl's Club in 1912 taken outside the Girls Club/Scout Hall on the Holcot Road. In 1928 the building was sold to the residents of Scaldwell, where it can still be seen, and the site used to build today's Village Hall.

Members of Brixworth Old Peoples' Welfare Association, or as they prefer to be called, 'The Evergreens' photographed at their first meeting in 1962 outside the Parish Hall on Northampton Road. The Hall was originally the home of The Salvation Army and the ground immediately outside became affectionately known as 'Alleluia Square'.

Brixworth & Scaldwell Cub pack photographed in the school playground, Church Street in 1956. From the left, back row, Nigel Wicks, Ricky Hadland, John Smallwood, Anthony Knight, David Gunnett, front row, Robert Wagg, Robin O'dell, Geoff Smith, Graham Smith and Tim Wilcox.

Derek Robinson, a Queen's Scout and Cub leader, with members of the Brixworth & Scaldwell pack sitting on the stocks in Church Street in the 1970's. The stocks were designed and made by local craftsmen Geoffrey Rowles and Dennis Mabbutt in the 1960's.

The Reverend Jack Burford, Vicar of All Saints' Church from 1952 to 1969, in the centre of the back row, with the male members of the choir in the late 1950's. Back row, from the left, Frank Cattell, Tony Thornton, Neville Campton (choirmaster), Rev Burford, Les Clarke, Len Hadland and Peter Bull.

Photograph of Brixworth Guides, Brownies and Cubs taken at the bottom of Cross Hill outside the rear entrance gates to the grounds of Brixworth Hall. The organisations may have been photographed together as part of their joint celebrations at the time of Queen Elizabeth II's Coronation in 1953.

A group of Brixworth ladies, members of the British Legion or the Women's Institute, photographed on a coach outing to the Wedgewood Pottery factory, Stoke-on-Trent, in the late 1930's. Many long established Brixworth families are represented here, with some of the ladies, their children, and their grandchildren living in the village today. The single male member of the group, in the centre towards the top, is believed to be the coach driver.

Members of Brixworth Women's Institute photographed in the Village Hall in 1973 following their 50th anniversary celebrations the previous year. The W.I. is one of the village's longest established organisations and it continues to flourish alongside many of the newer groups that have formed in more recent times.

A 1960's photograph of the Red Lion darts team and their partners ready to leave the pub's car-park for a visit to a show, compered by Bruce Forsyth at the London Palladium theatre. Many of those seen here and their families still live in the village.

Brixworth Boy's Club ready for a friendly game of cricket at Home Farm during the late 1940's. From the left, Don Amer, Alan Webb, Arthur Lade, Desmond Valentine, Phil Wright, John Booker, Bill Marsh and Tony Harris.

One of several pictures in this book depicting a village scene on 'Old Man Preston's' land where the Lone Pine Court flats now stand. This photograph shows members of Brixworth Lawn Tennis Club before a game during the 1930's.

Photograph courtesy of Kettering Evening Telegraph.

Brixworth's Badminton Club, winners of the Northamptonshire Junior League for the 1988-9 season, at their prize presentation in Wellingborough. From the left, back row, Robin Hodgson, Russell Parsons, Deene Copson, Debbie Reid (Barclaycard Sponsors), Jonathon Kirton, Paul Leeming, front row, Alison Kirton, Teresa White, Joanne Cuthbert, Hayley Lambert and Lindsey Allan.

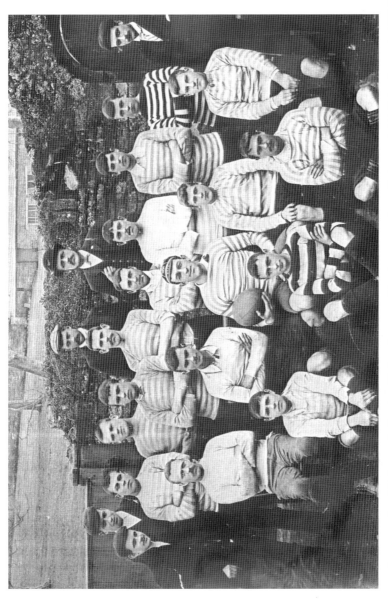

A rare team photograph of Brixworth Rugby Club taken outside the grounds to Brixworth Hall in the early 1900's. The club is thought to have stopped playing around the time of the First World War. Almost a hundred years later, in 1996, a new Rugby Club was formed in the village and it is likely the East Midlands R.F.U. will award it full league status before the year 2000.

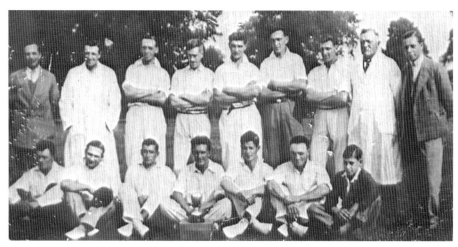

Brixworth's 1929 Cup winning cricket team photographed on the Holcot Road Recreation Ground. Regrettably the names of two members of the team cannot be recalled starting with the first player on the left of the back row. Standing next to him is Frank Cattell then Frank Adams, Walter Plowman, Bill Russell, Jack Unwin, Frank Tyrrell, John Buswell, Charles Sharpe, front row, Jack Buswell, Frank Simpson, Dick Walters, no name, Arthur Lyman, Bill Goodway and Sid Mumford.

Another Brixworth cup winning cricket team, this time from the 1940's, seen here on 'workhouse field', at Turney Brothers' Park Farm, Spratton Road. Captain Eric Wright is holding the trophy in the centre of the front row and Don Wastell, who contributed this photograph, is standing fourth from the left on the back row.

Brixworth's 1953 cricket team photographed on St. David's Playing Field. Back row, from the left, Jim Tite, Bert Maiden, Alf Cockerill, Dennis Smith, Tony Eldred, Eric Wright, Jack Barker, George Wilford, Jean Parrott (scorer), front row, Ralph Smith, Bernard Walker, Tom Smith, Oliver Kilby and Andy Desmond.

Members of Brixworth Cricket Club's Presidents Team in the summer of 1975. Standing, from the left, Tom Smith, Jack Bason, Roger Graves, Gordon Blake, Ian Launden, John Hurley, Ken Hudson, John Booker, Norman Tasker, front row, Dennis Mabbutt, Geoff Smith (captain), Jack Hostler, Jack Mayes and Barry Johnson.

Brixworth football team in 1920 photographed in front of the goal on their pitch at the recreation ground on the Holcot Road.

Brixworth All Saints' football team, seen here as the 1933-34 Mid Northants Village League Champions, photographed outside the Orangery of Brixworth Hall. Back row, form the left, F. Archer, W. Hiam, A. Dickens, J. Shirley, L. Martin, centre row, A. Cockerill, F. Tyrrell, J. Unwin, front row, A. Smith, R. Rose, G. Blake, J. Cook and W. Cockerill.

A late 1940's photograph of Brixworth football team taken on land belonging to Turney's farm with Northampton Road in the background. Back row, from the left, Alan Webb, Desmond Valentine, Joe Smith, Ken Barwell, Tony Wright, front row, Michael Chataway, Bill Marsh, Peter Blake, Robin Cliffe, Don Wastell and Roger Blake.

Early 1950's cup winning football team, which played in the Central Northants Combination League. Back row, from the left, Frank Tyrrell, Gordon Blake (Senior), Dick Hazelby, Peter Blake, Tom Nicholson, Morris Mabbutt, Jack Buswell, Lewis Horne, Don Amer, Frank Watkins, Don Wastell, Fred Archer, Ted Robinson, Will Bagguley, John Bell, front row, Robin Cliffe, Trevor Nicholson, Gordon Blake, Dennis Smith, Charlie Prior and Andy Desmond (mascot).

Brixworth football team photographed on St. David's Playing Field during the 1957-58 season which played in the Central Northants Combination League. Back row, from the left, Frank Letts, Mick Tobbutt, Don Amer, Ted Buck, Gordon Blake, Charlie Pryor, front row, Peter Cockerill, Geoff Wykes, Peter Eldred, John Blason and Phil Wright.

Brixworth's Senior and Junior cup winning football teams photographed at St. David's Playing Field at the end of the 1960-1 season. The boys sitting from the left, Dale Faulkner, Trevor Vials, Ian Buswell, Peter Robinson, David Brown, Ian Mayes, Steve Watkins, Kevin Eldred, Colin Dunn, Dave Maiden, Geoff Armiger, Steve Burdon and Kevin Crawley.

# Section 7
## Weddings

Brixworth's first parish register of marriages was produced in 1565 when the village name was spelt 'Brekelesworth'. In 1571 the spelling changed to 'Bryckelsworth' and it was sometime during the next hundred years that it took on the spelling we use today. The photographs chosen for this section were first seen in public in the summer of 1996 when they formed part of an exhibition of wedding photographs held in The Heritage Centre, organised by Brixworth History Society. It was fitting that this event was arranged to take place at the same time as the church's Flower Festival which also had the theme of 'Weddings'. The Festival ended with a special service during which married couples were given the opportunity to re-affirm their wedding vows. The clothes worn by the happy couples you are about to see provide a fascinating glimpse of the many changes that have taken place in wedding fashion since the beginning of the 20th century.

War bride Nancy Tyrrell with groom Ron Bounds who were married on 31st January 1942. Ron ran his own private hire taxi business in Brixworth for 36 years. His brother set up a similar taxi business in Northampton that is still operating today.

Evelyn Rose married Frank Cattell on 18th August 1903. The bride was the second daughter of George Rose, a well known local farmer. The wedding was conducted by the Vicar of All Saints' Church, The Reverend A. K. Pavey.

Evelyn's bridesmaids were Miss B. Rose, Miss N. Rose, Miss A. Mallard, Miss F. Dickens and Miss V. Rose. Mr. W. Gammage was the best man and Master R. Rose was the page boy.

Lavinia Marriott married Frank Lever on 1st June 1914. Lavinia was a nursery maid to the Paget family who lived for some time at Brixworth Hall and Frank was a farmer at Folly Farm.

Vera Rose and Percy Vivian at their marriage in the 1920's, photographed at Rookery Farm. Percy had his own haulage and motor engineering business based in Church Street and at Hall Farm. Vera's father was the publican at The Hare & Hounds in Church Street.

Hilda Mallard and William Atterbury married on 19th October 1933. The bride and groom were both from farming families and Hilda started the local Cubs group in Brixworth. The happy couple can be seen here leaving Brixworth Parish Church under an archway formed by members of the local cubs.

Brixworth's vicar The Reverend Joseph Palmer conducted the marriage service for Winifred Clements and Jack Dawson on 3rd August 1935. Jack was born in the village and worked for some time for the local builder Leslie Hamson.

Mabel Chapman and Horace Mash at their wedding in All Saints' Church on 21st August 1937. Mabel and Horace were the last couple married by the Reverend Palmer before his sudden death the following week.

Peggy Lever and Harry Mallard photographed at their wedding on 3rd November 1938. The bride and groom met during their school days and have lived in Brixworth all their lives. Harry's family has farmed in the village since the turn of the century.

Lilly Cattell and Oliver Kilby seen here at their wedding on 28th October 1939. Lilly was born in Brixworth and like several other women from the village she worked at a garment factory in Market Harborough. Gloucestershire born Oliver worked as a crane driver on the local ironstone quarries.

Bride Nancy Moody and groom Jack Whelan photographed at North Hall, Northampton Road (now the site of the Pytchley Court Nursing Home) on 9th November 1939. Nancy worked in a china shop in Northampton and her husband was in the police force.

Doris Evans and Charles Sharpe in the courtyard of The George Inn, Newlands, on their wedding day in October 1941. Doris' father and grandfather were both village blacksmiths with their workshop in Newlands. Their business closed down soon after the end of the Second World War. When Charles left school he worked as a groom for the Pytchley Hunt.

Doris Lade married Jack Mayes, seen here dressed in his Royal Airforce uniform, on 24th January 1942. From the 1930's Jack's father Harold owned the local 'paper shop', now Brixworth Stores, on Northampton Road. Jack and Doris, who was born and bred in the village, took over and ran the business from 1955 to 1967.

Iris Watkins and Cliff Bates married on 18th October 1947. Iris was chairman of Brixworth Parish Council for 10 years and a member of the District Council and Cliff, with his brother Ken, owned the butchers shop on the corner of Northampton Road and Kennel Terrace.

Beattie Glover and Arthur Wright at their wedding on 15th November 1947. Beattie was born in Brixworth and worked at the same garment factory as Lilly Cattell, whose photograph is on page 95. Arthur was also born in the village and his first job, after leaving school, was at Vivian's Garage in Church Street.

Mary Tyrrell married builder Len Billingham on 31st July 1948. Mary was born in Brixworth and worked at the Highfield laundry on the Northampton Road. Len's parents ran the Griffin public house in the nearby village of Pitsford.

Brixworth born Lillian Pearce and Derek Mabbutt seen here after their marriage service conducted by the Reverend Burford on 1st April 1961. Derek, from Holcot, worked as a builder and he and Lillian fostered over 30 children before they moved to Northampton in 1980.

# ACKNOWLEDGEMENTS

Books of this kind are impossible to produce without the help of a great number of people. As previously mentioned, most of the images we have used in this book are copies of photographs taken from the private collections of Brixworth residents, with much of the supporting text based upon the recollections of local people who have willingly shared their memories of 'Brixworth past' with us. It is to these people that our greatest thanks must go. We are also grateful to Geoffrey Starmer for allowing us to reprint his copyright photograph of the aerial ropeway on page 27 and to our main sponsor Ilmor Engineering for providing the images we have included on pages 24, 25 and 72 (bottom). The top photograph on page 71 and the bottom one on page 82 are courtesy of Northamptonshire Newspapers Ltd.

We have spent many months and several sleepless nights selecting the photographs, researching the facts and finally writing the text for this book, confident that our proof readers would correct any mistakes we have made. We are indebted to Tony Dawson, John Mills, Dick Walker, Basil Lockwood, Paddy Fox and Joan Mawby for checking our draft copy and making several important factual and grammatical changes for us.

Our thanks go to Northamptonshire's County Archivist Rachel Watson for writing a Foreword to the book and for the advice and encouragement she continues to give to our Society.

Finally we wish to express our gratitude again to our five business partners and the printers for providing the funds and expertise we needed to transform our collection of photographic images and memories into 'A Pictorial History of Brixworth'.

The Production Team - 'A Pictorial History of Brixworth'.

# BRIXWORTH HISTORY SOCIETY

Brixworth History Society was formed in 1990 following enormous interest shown in an exhibition of village photographs organised by local residents John and Mandy Dawkins the previous year. The group meet every month, except August, and has over fifty subscribing members. Activities include illustrated talks on a wide range of historical topics, guided tours and walks in and around Brixworth and an annual coach trip. The Society has organised two highly successful exhibitions and in 1993 published it's first book 'Brixworth Now and Then - A Village Walk'. More recently four members produced a perpetual calendar which, like the book, is a popular purchase for both local residents and those who visit the village.